THE LIBRARY OF
AMERICAN
LIVES AND TIMES™

ELI WHITNEY

The Cotton Gin and American Manufacturing

Regan A. Huff

BPMS MEDIA CENTER

The Rosen Publishing Group's
PowerPlus Books™
New York

For Bill Brown

Published in 2004 by The Rosen Publishing Group, Inc.
29 East 21st Street, New York, NY 10010

First Edition

Editor's Note: All quotations have been reproduced as they appeared in the letters and diaries from which they were borrowed. No correction was made to the inconsistent spelling that was common in that time period.

Library of Congress Cataloging-in-Publication Data

Huff, Regan A.
Eli Whitney : the cotton gin and American manufacturing / Regan A. Huff.
    p. cm. — (The library of American lives and times)
Includes bibliographical references and index.
ISBN 0-8239-6628-3
1. Whitney, Eli, 1765–1825. 2. Inventors—United States—Biography.
3. Cotton gins and ginning. I. Title. II. Series.
TS1570.W4 H84 2004
609.2—dc21

                              2002010256

Manufactured in the United States of America

CONTENTS

1. Introduction

In the early 1800s, during the later years of Eli Whitney's life, an influential friend wrote of the famous inventor, "Mr. Whitney is now employed in manufacturing muskets for the United States. In this business he has probably exceeded the efforts not only of his countrymen, but of the whole civilized world by a system of machinery of his own invention." Whitney emerged as a symbol not only of creative genius and intelligence but also of the American spirit of independence. The gun factory and farm that he owned became a travel destination. Americans brought foreign visitors to his factory to impress them with the neatness and organization of the machinery. The waterpower system that drove the machines, though no different in principle from those in use at factories all over the country, struck observers as somehow out of the ordinary, perhaps in its attention to how the machinery's stones were cut

---

Opposite: Samuel Morse's portrait of Eli Whitney, made circa 1822, shows the inventor in his study. Morse was a successful painter, but he is best known as the inventor of the telegraph machine and the telegraph language, Morse code. The two inventors were neighbors.

and shaped or in the beauty of the iron waterwheel in motion. One visitor was amazed by Whitney's storage shed because of the way carts could be pushed up a steep bank behind it and tipped to release their loads of coal into the shed to be stored. His barn was called a model of convenience. Even the cows, which wore special harnesses invented by Whitney, benefited from his ingenuity. People seemed to find signs of genius in everything that Whitney touched.

In the public mind, Whitney was a hero of manufacturing who triumphed over the world with his ability to build machines that allowed work to be done faster and more precisely. America needed a hero of Whitney's type to demonstrate that the country was the intellectual and manufacturing equal of any other nation. Most Europeans who traveled in early America described Americans as rough and backward, proud of their self-sufficiency and content to dress in coarse clothing, live in small villages, and do without the things that they could not make themselves. Whitney represented the power and potential of that same spirit of self-reliance. He did not have to do without. He believed that he could make anything himself, given the right tools. If he had to, he could even make the tools himself.

Whitney was a farmer's son who, by means of his own cleverness, rose to great heights. As a young boy in rural Massachusetts, he showed exceptional mechanical talent. To escape the life of a farmer, he went to college. To pay his college debts, he took a job in the South, where he encountered a problem that he thought he had the mechanical skills to solve. After an initial flash of insight, he produced the first rough model of his most famous invention, the cotton gin, in just ten days.

Whitney's gin changed the entire country. It made cleaning cotton faster and easier, which in turn made cotton profitable to grow. Cotton was soon the dominant crop in the South. In turn, the availability of inexpensive cotton helped the textile mills of the North to flourish, setting the scene for an industrial revolution. However, although Whitney was recognized for the genius of his invention, the design for his gin was stolen and copied. He spent years unsuccessfully chasing after the profit that he believed was his due.

Tired of struggling to pay his bills, he changed his course, putting his talents to use making muskets for the U.S. government. Not only was Whitney able to make money in his new business and live comfortably at last, his innovations in manufacturing and production helped to transform American industry. Ultimately, he helped to bring about a revolution in American manufacturing. Europeans came back to America to look in wonder at factories, eager to learn the secret of the highly advanced and successful American system of manufacturing.

2. Enterprising Youth

The British colonies of North America were rich in natural resources. For most of the seventeenth and eighteenth centuries, British colonists shipped lumber, fish, and agricultural products to Europe and to European colonies in the West Indies. Many American colonists made a profit as participants in this trade. They, in turn, purchased manufactured goods, including cloth, muskets, and iron tools, from Europe, because the industry to make these products did not yet exist in America.

As did most revolutionary-era farmers, Eli Whitney's father, also named Eli, had a workshop for making and repairing simple tools and farm equipment, and young Eli spent much of his free time in the shop, learning to make tools under his father's instruction. Eli had chores to do on the family's Westborough, Massachusetts, farm, including feeding and watering sixty cows, before going to school in the morning. He soon demonstrated that his talent and interest was in the workshop, not on the farm. Even as a young boy, Eli was a skilled craftsman, and he was beginning to show a drive to put his skills to use.

By the time Eli celebrated his fourteenth birthday, the American Revolution had been going on for four years. The Revolution (1775–1783) disrupted the traditional trade pattern between Britain and its American colonies. Great Britain imposed trade restrictions, which threatened both American merchants and European countries that did business with American merchants. Colonists, no longer able to import many raw materials and manufactured goods, were limited to what they could make themselves.

Eli saw the wartime shortages of imported goods as an opportunity rather than as an obstacle. Eli set up a small forge for heating and shaping iron, and the young

Eli Whitney would have outfitted his small forge with some of the simple tools of a colonial blacksmith, including a hammer, a file, a pair of tongs, and an anvil. Iron, heated yellow-hot by the coal fire that burned in the brick hearth, would have been hammered and filed into shape. The scene would have looked like the blacksmith shop shown above, which is a working re-creation located in Colonial Williamsburg.

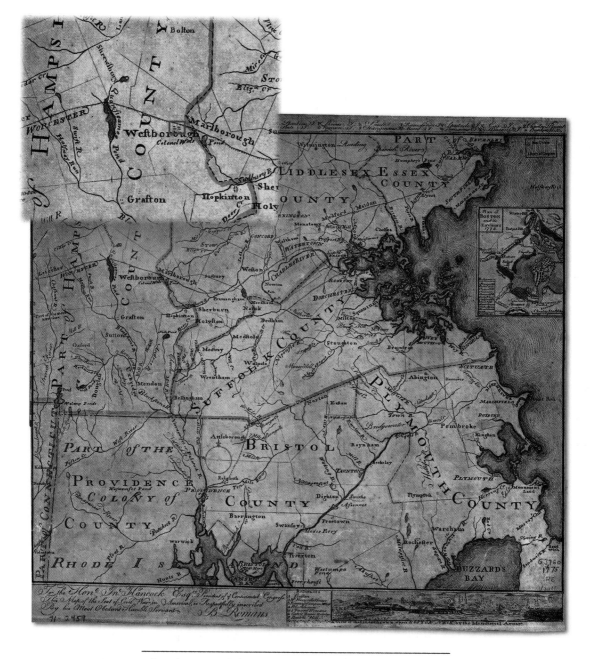

During Eli Whitney's lifetime, Westborough, Massachusetts, was a medium-size farming community, boasting about 100 families by the mid-eighteenth century. The town also was home to many taverns and inns, which offered shelter and rest to travelers on the way to Boston. Bernard Romans created this hand-colored map in 1775. The town of Westborough is indicated by a blue box *(inset)*.

boy began his first commercial venture: making crude nails and selling them to local farmers, merchants, and craftsmen for building everything from farm equipment to houses.

Eli ran his little business for two years. Soon he was also fixing the metal tools of neighboring farmers and struggling to meet the demand for homemade nails. Recognizing that there was more demand for nails than he could meet, Eli set out to recruit hired help. He vanished for three days and returned home with an assistant who would work in Eli's forge for three months. With the help of a hired assistant, Eli was able to meet the demand for nails, and, despite paying the assistant a regular salary, he was still able to make a profit.

Although he was probably one of the youngest to seize upon its potential, Eli was not the only person to recognize this business opportunity. During the war, many farmers set up small forges to make nails. Eli Whitney, however, was one of the few to anticipate what would happen when the war came to an end. After the American Revolution, Great Britain had a surplus of nails that had gone unsold during the war. When the doors of trade between Britain and North America were once again open, cheap British nails flooded the American market, and the demand for home-forged, American nails disappeared. Eli switched to a new product. He began manufacturing hatpins, long, sharp pieces of metal that kept ladies' hats firmly secured to their hair. Eli Whitney had a talent for making things with his hands, and he had good business sense. He understood how to adapt his industry to changes in the market.

Eli's father was proud of his son's success. Eli's stepmother, Judith, was less enthusiastic. Eli's mother had died when he was eleven, and his father had remarried several years later. Eli treated Judith with respect, but he did not have a warm relationship with her. In turn, Judith may have been jealous of the praise that Eli received for his mechanical talents. It is very likely that young Eli neglected his farm chores in favor of his forge, and this also may have bothered his stepmother.

Eli had great confidence in his abilities and did not mind letting others know it. His stepmother was fond of a set of knives that she owned, and Eli's sister Elizabeth remembered him bragging, "I can make just such ones if I had tools and I could make tools if I had tools to make them with." Today, it is rare for people in America to make their own tools to do a job, but in Eli's day it was often necessary. Specialized tools were not usually available for sale in stores. Mechanical ability included not only using tools or machines but also imagining, designing, and building a tool that could perform a particular task. A few months after Eli made his boast, Judith broke one of her prized knives. Eli followed through on his claim, making a new knife that matched the rest of the set beautifully.

Seeing Eli's obvious skill, Judith accepted the family's view of his talents.

At the age of nineteen, Eli made a declaration that surprised his family. He wanted to go to college. In Eli's time, most college students came from wealthy families, whereas the Whitneys were small-scale farmers. Furthermore, America's few colleges trained book-smart politicians, lawyers, and ministers and seemed to have little to offer a mechanically gifted young man. Eli lacked both the preparation and the money he would need, but he was determined to go. He did not like farming, and if he wanted a different kind of life he needed a plan that would get him out of Westborough. His stepmother was firmly against the idea of Eli going to college. She was probably concerned about the sacrifices that the family would have to make to provide the needed funds. Eli's father withheld his opinion, waiting to see how Eli would attempt to achieve his goal.

Eli had attended school regularly during his youth, but his local grammar school did not teach advanced Latin, Greek, and mathematics, subjects he would need to study to be accepted into college. Eli would need to enroll in an academy, an institution established to prepare students for higher education. Academies were springing up all over New England, but it cost money to attend them. Eli decided to get a job as a schoolmaster during the winter to pay for his study at Leicester Academy in the summer.

The Lyons Farm schoolhouse was built in 1784, in the town of Newark, New Jersey. It is typical of the kind of one-room schools that were built throughout the northeast during the eighteenth century. The Grafton schoolhouse where Eli Whitney worked as a teacher would have looked very similar to this one.

His father expressed doubt that Eli was qualified for a teaching job, but Eli insisted that he could manage to keep a few weeks ahead of his students. To his father's surprise, the town of Grafton, Massachusetts, hired twenty-year-old Eli Whitney as a schoolmaster in the winter of 1785. Eli's salary was small, but it was enough to cover his tuition at Leicester Academy the following spring. Through the next four years, he improved as both a teacher and a scholar. As a boy, Eli had been quick with numbers but had had trouble

As an application for a teaching position at a local grammar school, Eli Whitney provided this writing sample, which reads "To the Selectmen of Westborough. Gentlemen, you are undoubtedly acquainted with my Reputation, and as for my Penmanship it must speak for itself; this is to desire your Approbation to keep a public School. These from your humble Servant, Eli Whitney Junr."

When Eli Whitney was a boy, almost all Americans lived in rural communities of less than 2,500 residents. In the North, a rural district would usually build a single-room school. The district would scrape together money from property taxes and student fees to hire a schoolmaster and would depend on donations of wood or coal to heat the school during winter. Students spent time memorizing lessons and were expected to recite rules of grammar and arithmetic. Subjects such as social studies and science were not generally taught. Most children under fourteen attended school at least occasionally during the year. In the South, schoolmasters traveled around like salesmen, offering their services as teachers. Sometimes parents organized "old-field schools" on land no longer used for farming and engaged schoolmasters to teach. Wealthier families might hire a tutor to stay at their home and teach only their children. Across the country, academies were being established. Students who were able to pay the tuition could continue beyond the district or old-field school and prepare for entrance into one of America's handful of colleges. Few students in Whitney's era, however, had the desire or the money to acquire this much education.

Ebenezar Crafts and Jacob Davis founded Leicester Academy in 1784. When Whitney enrolled in the school the following summer, the entire institution was housed in a single building, the former mansion of a local businessman named Aaron Lopez. This academy building, shown above, would contain the school's dormitory, dining hall, and classrooms for the next twenty years.

learning to read. In preparation for college, Eli worked diligently to improve his grasp of ancient languages. Eli's sister later recalled that an academy teacher told their father that Eli was "an excellent schollar and ought by all means to go to colledge."

Finally, Eli's father was won over and agreed to provide his son with money for college. Eli decided to apply for admission to Yale College in New Haven, Connecticut. By letter, perhaps with the recommendation of the Leicester Academy headmaster, who was a

Yale graduate, Eli arranged an appointment with Yale's president, the Reverend Ezra Stiles. The two men would meet for the personal interview that would determine whether or not Eli was qualified to enroll in Yale College. In early March 1789, Eli's father took him by sleigh as far as an inn in Brookfield, Massachusetts, where they stayed overnight. The following morning, the younger Whitney caught a stagecoach heading south to Connecticut.

3. College Man

Eli Whitney did not go straight to New Haven and Yale. He stopped first in Durham, Connecticut, a town to the north of New Haven, where he was able to make final preparations for the entrance exam under the supervision of the Reverend Elizur Goodrich. Reverend Goodrich was an accomplished mathematician who had almost become president of Yale, stepping aside in favor of his friend Ezra Stiles. Goodrich became a friend to whom Eli could turn for assistance and wise advice. He wrote letters of recommendation on behalf of Eli to other influential Yale graduates and later owned a house in New Haven where Eli boarded and ate meals with the Goodrich family.

More than a month after he arrived in Durham, Eli Whitney set off for New Haven, ready to meet with Ezra Stiles. The examination began at 9:00 A.M. and continued until 2:00 P.M. Eli had to translate pages in Latin and Greek and show a knowledge of the rules of arithmetic. As Stiles talked with the twenty-three-year-old prospective freshman, the college president also

Yale graduate Ezra Stiles served as president of the college
from 1777 until his death in 1795. Stiles was a pastor,
a professor, and a writer. Though a profoundly religious man,
Stiles introduced modern sciences to the Yale curriculum.
This oil portrait was painted by Reuben Moulthrop.

looked for evidence of good character. At the end of the day, he was impressed enough to admit Whitney to Yale College immediately.

Whitney became one of perhaps two hundred students at Yale being educated by a handful of tutors, professors, and the Reverend Stiles. College was rigorous. There were strict rules about what students studied and how they spent their time. After attending chapel early in the morning, students had to recite material that they had studied and memorized the

Yale students enjoy a moment of leisure in a 1910 etching of the campus based on A. P. Doolittle's 1807 engraving. Originally founded as the Collegiate School in Abraham Pierson's Killingworth, Connecticut, home, the school moved to New Haven in 1716. In 1718, merchant Elihu Yale made a donation of books and other goods, and the college was renamed for him.

The first American colleges were sponsored by the church. A decade before Eli Whitney entered Yale, biblical scholarship was the core of all academic study. Nearly all college professors were ministers. The young men of Yale typically spent Monday and Tuesday studying philosophy, Wednesday studying Greek, Thursday studying the languages of the Bible, and Friday working on English composition. Math and science were seen as fairly unimportant. In Europe, however, a trend in scholarship known as the Enlightenment was producing discoveries that would lead to the fields of physics, biology, chemistry, and geology. Some Americans felt that an educated man needed to understand these new sciences, but they were not yet part of the traditional course of study. When Whitney entered Yale, the study of ancient languages and texts remained important, but science was becoming a major component of the standard curriculum. Ezra Stiles was a minister, but he was also interested in the natural world and its principles. Stiles hired a professor of mathematics and experimental science who was not a minister in the church. Within Whitney's lifetime, Yale hired another science professor, a chemist and geologist, so that two of the college's five professors taught math and science.

night before. They would recite for the college tutors several more times during the day or would participate in public debates that demonstrated the knowledge gained through study. Students depended on books from the college library for even their core studies, because few young men could have afforded the texts. Whitney made particularly good use of the library, which housed 2,700 volumes, more books than he had ever seen.

Yale also had a museum that housed scientific equipment. During Eli Whitney's years at Yale, the museum grew with Revernd Stiles's support. Ezra Stiles ordered instruments from Europe, including a telescope, a model of the solar system that showed the motions of the planets, and a micrometer for taking very small measurements. Yale's collection already included mechanical devices, such as an air pump, a spouting fountain, and models of simple machines. Whitney would have been able to

This 1734 microscope was added to Yale's collection of scientific instruments as the college expanded its curriculum to include the natural sciences.

Yale's Connecticut Hall, built in the 1750s, is New Haven's oldest surviving building. Constructed as a dormitory for first-year students, it was home to famous Yale graduates Nathan Hale, Samuel Morse, Noah Webster, and Eli Whitney. The building now houses the university's philosophy and literature departments.

examine all of these instruments and to study their workings, but his education at Yale primarily focused on ancient languages, philosophy, and debate.

Colleges for mechanically talented students that emphasized the study of science and math did not appear in America until the 1820s. Had he been born a few decades later, Whitney might have attended one of these technical institutes, where he would have been able to study mechanical principles and applied chemistry instead of Greek and Hebrew. However, even if his studies at Yale were not suited to his interests in science and math, the relationships he formed with his professors and classmates served him well in life. In addition to his skill in the classroom, Whitney proved an able student of human nature and gentlemanly habits. He adopted the dress and manners of his peers at Yale and was popular with his classmates. He was at times on equal terms with friends from families of higher social standing or greater wealth. Whitney's natural charm and quick conversation were made even more effective by the polish he received at Yale. His education made him a persuasive speaker and writer, and these skills perhaps benefited him more than any of the specific knowledge that he gained from his formal studies.

4. Going South

When Eli Whitney finished his studies at Yale, he was in debt. He owed money for room, board, clothing, and other expenses, and he wrote to his father begging for help. His father had no money to spare and even warned Whitney that, whether he entered into business or continued to study further after college, he would have to support himself. Whitney's first intention was to pay his debts. He thought he might get a teaching position in New York City, but it fell through. Then Phineas Miller, a Yale graduate and the manager of a Georgian plantation owned by a woman named Catherine Greene, told Ezra Stiles about a position available for a private tutor at a plantation near another of Greene's estates, in South Carolina. Stiles recommended Eli Whitney, and Miller hired him on behalf of the South Carolinian. Whitney arranged to meet Miller in New York City, where the two men would join Catherine Greene on the voyage south.

Whitney eagerly calculated that, in his new position, he would be paid well enough to save 50 guineas per year and be out of debt in a short time. He was still

Phineas Miller's signature appeared on countless documents over the course of his long friendship and professional partner-ship with fellow Yale graduate Eli Whitney. The example shown above, which reads "I am Sir, your obedient & humble Ser[van]t. Phin. Miller," is taken from a letter written to Whitney on September 20, 1792.

young and inexperienced, however, and he had never lived anywhere but Massachusetts and Connecticut. The American Southeast was a distant and unfamiliar destination for residents of New England, and it had a reputation for being an unhealthy place. Whitney had heard many stories of gentlemen who traveled south and died from illnesses caught in the hot, humid climate. With some misgivings, Whitney boarded a packet ship bound for New York City, perhaps aware that his life was about to change.

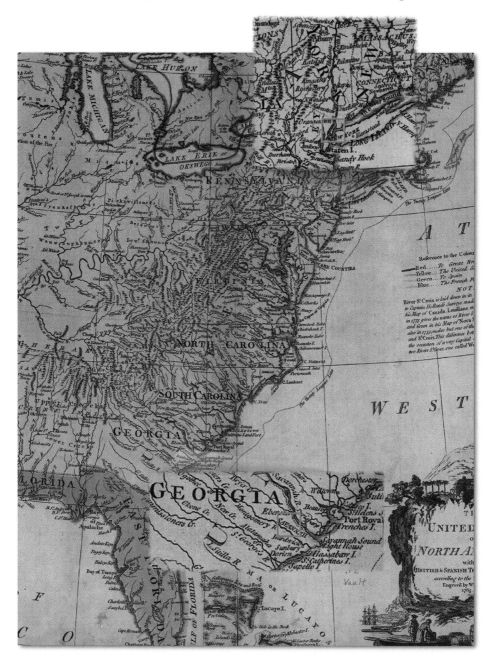

Though increasingly settled by northerners seeking new opportunities, the South was still an isolated, unfamiliar place in the early 1790s. The trip by ship from New York City *(indicated by a blue box in the inset at top)* to Savannah *(indicated by a green box in the inset at bottom)* was a difficult journey.

Arriving in New York City, Whitney marvelled at the bustling city. He wrote to his best friend, Josiah Stebbins, whom he had met at Leicester Academy, about the ships that he could watch coming in and going out of the busy harbor, and he mentioned that his time in New York was split between seeing the city and visiting with Catherine Greene's family. While exploring New York, Eli Whitney encountered and shook hands with an acquaintance who Whitney then realized was covered with the large, red sores of smallpox. Whitney rushed to a doctor and was given a smallpox inoculation to keep Whitney from getting a serious case of the deadly disease. Still not entirely recovered from his

During Eli Whitney's lifetime, cities were the breeding grounds of deadly diseases. Many people lived close together in cramped and often dirty dwellings, so diseases spread easily from one person to the next. Newcomers carrying viruses could spark new outbreaks. When Whitney got to New York, an outbreak of smallpox was raging. The only protection against the disease was called inoculation. A doctor would take a sample from the sores of an infected person and inject it into the body of a healthy person, who would then get a mild case of the disease, recover quickly, and be thereafter immune, or able to be exposed to the virus and not get sick.

A 1797 watercolor by John Joseph Holland depicts lower Manhattan, with City Hall in the distance. In 1790, slightly more than thirty-three thousand people lived in New York City. By 1800, that figure had nearly doubled, thanks to foreign immigration and American migration. This rapid growth brought with it disease and crime.

encounter with smallpox, Whitney set sail from New York, and, according to some accounts, became very seasick during his journey south. Catherine Greene graciously invited Whitney to stay at Mulberry Grove, her plantation in Georgia, to relax before traveling on to his new job in South Carolina.

Whitney accepted her invitation. Catherine Greene was the beautiful, energetic, and refined widow of General Nathanael Greene, a famous hero of the American Revolution. Both the general and his wife

Nineteen-year-old Catherine Littlefield married Nathanael Greene in July 1774. Their twelve-year marriage, which ended with Nathanael's death in 1786, was a happy one, and the couple had five children. After Nathanael's death, Catherine struggled to support her children and the large estate she inherited from her husband. She is shown here in middle age in an oil painting by James Frothingham.

had grown up in Rhode Island. Nathanael had educated himself in his family's anchor-making business, had been elected to the state legislature, and had been appointed to command Rhode Island's troops in the war. He had advanced in rank through his brilliantly organized campaigns, eventually becoming commander of the entire southern department of the war. Catherine had accompanied her husband and General George Washington and his troops during the winter that they had spent at Valley Forge, Pennsylvania. She had earned Washington's admiration for the way she kept up everyone's spirits during difficult times. General Greene's last great battle in the war had freed Charleston, South Carolina, from British occupation. Entering the recaptured city, Greene's hungry troops had wanted to steal food from shops and homes to add to the meager rations provided by the underfunded army. To prevent his men from committing theft, Greene had signed notes that made him personally responsible for paying back the cost of food taken by his troops. Greene had become a nationally recognized hero, but he was burdened with heavy debts for the expenses in Charleston, which he was never able to convince the U.S. government to repay.

General Greene's one reward had come from the grateful states of South Carolina and Georgia. These new state governments had given Greene land that had been confiscated, or taken away, from people who had remained loyal to the British government and who had been punished as traitors after the American victory. Mulberry Grove, a gift from the state of Georgia, was a beautiful piece of property along the Savannah River, although it had been abandoned for ten years when the Greenes arrived. In writing to a friend in Rhode Island, General Greene had described the plantation as having a magnificent house, a coach house and stables, an outdoor kitchen, a smokehouse, a chicken coop, a pigeon house with space for one thousand pigeons, and a large garden. General and Catherine Greene had made much-needed repairs and had planted crops to sustain themselves and to make money that could be put toward paying off their debt.

Mulberry Grove was mainly a rice plantation, as were many of the plantations along the low-lying coastal rivers of South Carolina and Georgia. Rice needs to be under freshwater during part of its growing cycle. Southern rice planters filled and drained their rice fields with the rise and fall of the rivers. The rivers' waters fill and drain with the tides of the ocean. A great deal of human labor was required to maintain the waterways and tide gates and to harvest and process the rice. The Greenes had 130 black slaves living and working at Mulberry Grove. In June 1786, while out with his laborers in the rice fields, General Greene had suffered sunstroke, or possibly a heart attack, and had died.

This undated sketch shows scenes from a southern rice plantation. At left, men dig ditches to carry water to the fields. At right, the rice is harvested by a group of women. In the center, a white overseer watches laborers in the fields. Below, the fields are flooded with water. Soon after his arrival in Savannah, Eli Whitney would have been familiar with ditches, floodgates, and mills like those illustrated in this sketch.

Catherine Greene had been left a widow with substantial debts, five young children, and a rice plantation. She had turned to Phineas Miller for help. Miller had graduated from Yale in 1785, and had come to Mulberry Grove to work as General Greene's secretary and to tutor his children. After General Greene's death, Miller had become the manager of the plantation and had helped Catherine Greene to maintain Mulberry Grove and continue to pay off her late husband's debts.

When he met Miller in New York, Whitney liked him almost immediately and judged him to be a man of character. Whitney was also very charmed by Catherine Greene. More than ten years Whitney's senior, Catherine had a strong spirit and a great deal of social grace. She created a comfortable society around her and probably knew how to choose her guests and to keep an evening enjoyable and lively. Her letters were warm and playful. She drew Whitney into the circle of her family and friends and made the young Whitney welcome in their company.

Phineas Miller and Catherine Greene soon became aware of Whitney's mechanical talents. When the three travelers reached Mulberry Grove, Miller's and Greene's encouragement and Whitney's genius bound the three together in a lifelong partnership that would change the face of America.

5. Conquering Cotton

By the end of the sixteenth century, Spanish, British, French, Dutch, and Danish entrepreneurs had begun to build busy ports of call and thriving estates on the Caribbean islands of the West Indies. During the next two hundred years, European colonists in the West Indies, who became both farmers and businessmen, proved that the tropical islands could be a profitable place. Following the example of the Portuguese colonies in Brazil, they established the plantation system, a way of making money from land through the intensive farming of a single crop. Sugarcane was the cash crop in the West Indies. It was boiled down into molasses for easier transport and was sold in Europe and North America.

The intensive production of sugarcane in the West Indies depended on large amounts of human labor, which created a demand for slaves. The slave trade involved many nations and groups. Several European countries established trade centers along the west coast of Africa. Many Africans, victims of the slave trade, were kidnapped in raids, were taken to the coast, and were sold to

English artist John Berryman traveled extensively in the West Indian island of Jamaica during the first years of the nineteenth century. Berryman documented the lives of African slaves in the colonial outpost. This woman is beating cassava, a fleshy root vegetable, into a juicy paste that can be used for a variety of domestic purposes.

slave traders who carried them against their will across the sea, where they were forced into labor, often on plantations. Other Africans profited from the slave trade as middlemen who captured Africans from weaker tribes and sold them to European traders in return for European manufactured goods. Still other African kingdoms managed to remain uninvolved.

During the next two hundred years, the colonial plantation system and the West Indian slave trade were adopted in the first American colonies. In 1619, the first African slaves were brought to the colony of Virginia. By 1790, the slave population in America had risen dramatically. The first federal census counted nearly 660,000 slaves in the American South.

Plantations were businesses. Southerners had land but hoped for wealth, and, if they wanted to make money as farmers, they needed to find a crop to grow and sell for a profit to fellow countrymen or to Europeans. Virginia's earliest colonists discovered that the climate and geography of the colony was particularly suited to growing tobacco, an important cash crop. The tobacco trade helped the struggling colony at Jamestown to become a permanent settlement. As colonies developed farther south, in South Carolina and Georgia, planters learned that the climate was too hot for tobacco but not hot enough for sugarcane. As late as 1790, Georgian and South Carolinian landowners were still eager to expand their agricultural interests with new cash crops.

When Eli Whitney arrived in Georgia, rice was the latest, greatest agricultural experiment, but it was hard to grow anywhere but on the banks of the rivers near the coast where the rise and fall of the tide watered and drained the crops. Farmers continued to experiment with other crops. Just three years before Whitney's arrival, seeds harvested from a foreign variety of cotton were planted for the first time in America on an island just off the Georgian coast. The cotton was known as long-staple cotton. It had been grown in India since ancient times, and, for centuries, a simple device called a *churka* had been used to remove the

The churka, or roller gin, is a simple machine. Turning a crank rotates two rollers, one made of wood and the other of iron. Seed cotton is fed into the small space between the two turning rollers. The cotton fiber is pinched and pulled through the rollers, but the seeds are too large to fit. Torn from the cotton fiber, the seeds fall to the ground.

smooth, black seeds from the puff of white fiber picked by hand from the plant. Seeds were removed so that the clean fibers could be made into cloth. The long-staple cotton grew well on Georgia's coast, and planters in Georgia began to get excited. Textile factories in Great Britain had developed new machines to manufacture cotton cloth faster, so the demand for raw cotton was growing. To the disappointment of Georgian planters, however, the easily processed long-staple cotton would only grow in a narrow strip of land along the Atlantic coast. The long-staple cotton refused to grow farther inland.

Some planters experimented with growing a different kind of cotton, a variety known as short-staple, or green-seed, cotton. It thrived, even on the higher ground of inland Georgia. This success, however, only led to another disappointment. Short-staple cotton turned out to be a lot harder to clean than the long-staple variety. Churkas were useless in removing the rough, green seeds from the cotton fiber. The crop could not be sold to textile factories unless the seeds were removed. Planters ordered their laborers to pick the seeds out by hand, but the process was too slow to be financially worthwhile. Dejected, planters let whole fields of green-seed cotton stand and wither on the stalk.

The problem of removing the seeds from green-seed cotton was very much on the minds of the Georgian planters that Eli Whitney met at Catherine Greene's house at Mulberry Grove. If someone could figure out a way to clean the short-staple cotton efficiently, the land in the interior of Georgia could be cleared and planted in cotton, the crop could be processed, and the raw cotton could be sold to British merchants or to the textile mills being built in the northeastern United States. The possibilities for wealth seemed limitless, and Georgian planters were eager to seize the opportunity.

While recuperating and relaxing in the comfortable surroundings of Mulberry Grove, Whitney idly turned the planters' problem over in his mind. Suddenly, he envisioned how he could build a machine that would do the work of cleaning the seeds from the cotton. In a single moment, Whitney changed the course of his own life. He did not go to South Carolina to teach. He stopped sending letters back to his father and Josiah Stebbins, normally his regular correspondents. Something big was happening, and Whitney was either too busy or too nervous to write about it.

The machine that Whitney designed is simple. Cotton picked from the stalk with the seeds still attached is fed into a hopper on one side of a large, wooden box. Turning a crank rotates a wheel inside the box. The wheel is covered with wire hooks, which catch the cotton fibers and draw them away from the sticky, green seeds. As the wheel turns, the fibers are pulled through a grate and emerge at the other end of the machine, where they are pulled free from the cylinder

Eli Whitney.

Cotton Gin

March 14, 1794

and its hooks by a rotating brush that Whitney called the clearer. The seeds are too wide to pass through the grate and instead fall to the floor. The seeds and the fiber are cleanly separated, with less labor than is required by picking out the seeds by hand or by using existing roller gins modeled on the Indian churka. In a letter to his father, Whitney later claimed that one man, with the help of a horse to power the gin, could clean as much cotton with his new gin as fifty men could clean with the old machines.

Whitney trusted Phineas Miller with his idea, and Miller offered him a deal. Whitney would build and test his machine to see if it would work, and Miller would pay all of his expenses. The two men would split any profits that the machine might bring. Whitney's options were somewhat limited. He was a man with an idea but without money. He could accept the offers made to him to buy the design of the machine outright for 100 guineas, the equivalent of his yearly salary, and leave the development and sale of the invention to someone else. He could keep his job as a tutor in South Carolina and work for several years to pay off his debts before trying to launch his invention with his own funds. He sensed, however, that he could not afford to wait. The need for

---

Opposite: Eli Whitney's sketch of his model cotton gin, which shows a cutaway side view *(top)* and an overhead view *(bottom)*, is dated March 14, 1794. The sketch was prepared to accompany his patent application for the invention.

---

the ginning machine was great at that moment. If he delayed, some other inventor with some other design might easily capture the market. Whitney seized the opportunity offered to him by Miller. Eventually, the two men formalized this partnership as the firm of Miller & Whitney.

Miller was responsible for raising money for the project. He looked to his southern connections to finance the costs of starting a cotton gin factory. Indirectly, Catherine Greene was a key investor, allowing her estate to be mortgaged, or used as a security, for the loans that the new business needed. Whitney did not think he could find skilled workmen in the South, so he decided to go back to New Haven and establish his factory there. His responsibility in the partnership was to gain a patent on his invention and gather the workmen, tools, and machines needed to produce a large number of cotton gins.

Instead of trying to sell the cotton gins, however, Miller and Whitney planned to sell the service of cotton ginning. Whitney knew that he could not, in a short time, make enough cotton gins to meet the demand of southern planters, and the partners calculated that the price they would have to charge for each gin would be too high for most cash-poor southern planters to pay. In addition, the firm wanted to be in complete control of the development of the industry and to benefit financially from its success. Miller intended to look for sites

Account of Miller & Whitney's Debts
Assumed by E. Whitney 1798.—

Amt. due N.H. Bank	4685	0
Interest 7 years & 2 mos	2913	30
	7598	30
Jere.t Atwaters note	112	—
Timothy Gorhams ..	27	87
Wm. Wallace ..	159	—
Jos. Gorham ..	25	—
Jacob Thompson ..	11	67
Benj.a Whitney ..	400	—
Joseph Lathrop ..	206	67
J & D Townsend ..	107	58
Solomon Fowler ..	28	34
Jesse Turner ..	159	—
Wm Mix ..	163	47
Do Do acct ..	42	88
Saml Houghton ..	108	90
Do ..	200	59
Abram Bassett ..	61	96
Joel Bishop ..	94	71
Street & Hughs ..	42	22
Do Do ..	87	76
Do Do ..	38	50
Thos Hawell ..	106	22
Phelps & Stanford ..	470	—
	2654	34
Int. y yrs & 2 mos ..	1596	5
	4250	39

Phineas Miller was successful in raising money from southern investors, but the initial operating expenses were great and soon threatened to bankrupt the business. A page, dated 1798, from the account books of Miller & Whitney includes a partial list of the company's many outstanding debts, which were to be assumed by Eli Whitney alone.

in the *Gazette of the State of Georgia,* encouraging farmers to plant green-seed cotton. He promised that the firm of Miller & Whitney would be able to gin any cotton that the farmers might produce. Miller selected a site near Augusta, Georgia, for the firm's first ginning operation and found a man to construct the buildings necessary for storing and ginning the cotton sure to arrive at harvest time. Whitney arrived in May with his first set of ginning machines.

The response to Miller's notice was overwhelming. The partners were unprepared for the demand. By late

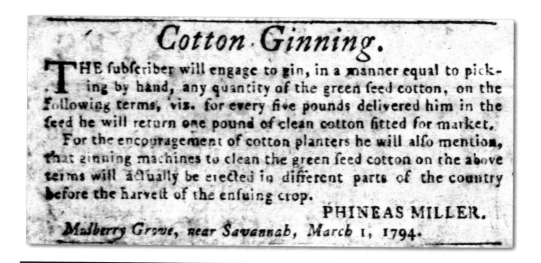

Phineas Miller's advertisement appeared in the *Gazette of the State of Georgia* on March 1, 1794. It read: "The subscriber will engage to gin, in a manner equal to picking by hand, any quantity of the green seed cotton . . . [F]or every five pounds delivered to him in the seed he will return one pound of clean cotton fitted for market."

On November 16, 1793, Thomas Jefferson, then serving as secretary of state, wrote to Eli Whitney, asking several questions about the quality and cost of his new invention, the cotton gin. Jefferson wrote, "I feel a considerable interest in the success of your invention. . . . Favorable answers to these questions would induce me to engage one of them to be forwarded to Richmond for me." Jefferson's enthusiasm reflected the widespread interest in Whitney's invention.

summer, the gins Whitney had built were already at work, beginning to clean the 800,000 pounds (362,873.9 kg) of cotton that had been grown, harvested, and stored in previous years. Whitney estimated that when the planters' fall harvest for 1794 was delivered, Miller & Whitney would need to clean upward of 5,000 pounds (2,268 kg) of cotton per day. Yet even when the firm reached its peak capacity, in 1796, Miller & Whitney's gins, scattered across Georgia, were only able to handle about 2,500 pounds (1,134 kg) per day.

The firm, still in its first year of existence, was overextended. Whitney worked hard to build as many gins as possible, sure that he could conquer the difficulties of large-scale manufacturing. He chose a factory site in New Haven, and Miller financed its purchase. As the first buildings of the factory were being constructed, Whitney hired workmen and began systematizing the way that they built the gins. Whitney returned to New Haven in March 1795, after a short trip to New York, and, to his horror, found his main factory building reduced to ashes. When the fire had broken out, his workmen had been at breakfast. No one had been hurt, but neither had anyone been around to save anything from the burning building. Whitney lost not only the shop itself, but also his special tools, machines, and twenty nearly completed cotton gins, which were all desperately needed in Georgia. Whitney had to begin again.

By fall 1795, the firm was in trouble financially. Because they had decided to set up ginning mills instead of simply selling manufactured gins, Miller and Whitney had to pay many substantial start-up expenses before ever making any money. Whitney had the expense of a workshop, land, tools, materials, and workmen to build the gins in Connecticut. In addition, the operations in Georgia required the purchase of land, the construction of buildings, and the employment of labor for each of the ginneries. All this had to be done before a single pound of cotton could be ginned. Miller had mortgaged Mulberry Grove and other parts of Catherine Greene's estate to establish the credit he needed to cover these costs, but the firm needed more money than he could borrow.

Whitney found his own sources of credit in New Haven to replace his tools and to reconstruct his machines. He continued to build cotton gins in the buildings remaining on his factory site, but competition was successfully encroaching on Miller & Whitney's potential profits. Other entrepreneurs did not sit still while Miller & Whitney struggled to meet demand and keep their exclusive hold on the ginning business, and several variations of Whitney's gin appeared for sale in Georgia. Miller publicly called for a stop to these patent infringements, but unless he could successfully sue one of the violators, no one would listen. Many planters preferred to buy gins illegally copied from Whitney's

An entrepreneur needs money, or capital, to create a business and to begin operations. Start-up money usually comes in the form of a loan or a line of credit. If all goes well, the business will succeed and make money before the loan has to be repaid. The entrepreneur is then able to pay back the loan, along with an extra charge known as interest, using part of the business's profits. Today, entrepreneurs can either get a business loan from a bank or sell their idea to an organized group of investors. In Whitney's day, the process of obtaining credit to start a business was less formal. Banks did not yet function as lending institutions for individuals. Credit arrangements were personal, and people faced personal bankruptcy if their businesses failed. Phineas Miller, who was established in Georgia as a reputable man, approached gentlemen he knew in the area and asked them for loans. Miller's creditors hoped to realize a profit, in the form of interest, if the business did well, but they also trusted Miller's honor to guarantee that they would be paid back no matter what happened.

patented model and to hide them away on their own plantations rather than pay Miller & Whitney a substantial fee each time they had cotton that needed to be cleaned. In addition, a new snag arose. Some of the cleaned short-staple cotton arriving in Great Britain was rejected by British mills. British spinners feared that the shorter fibers might not work in British spinning machinery. Although the shorter fibers were later shown to be just as good as the long-staple cotton the spinners had long used, the incident brought bad press for the firm of Miller & Whitney. In Georgia, rumors spread that it was Miller & Whitney's ginning that had caused the cotton to be rejected.

Phineas Miller traveled to New Haven in the fall of 1795 to tell Whitney that Whitney needed to travel to England, smooth out the difficulties over the purchase of cleaned green-seed cotton, and perhaps seek British patent rights to the invention while he was there. Miller had respect for Whitney's abilities as a diplomat and thought that he could successfully demonstrate to British textile manufacturers that the short-staple cotton appearing on the market from the American South was as good as the long-staple cotton the manufacturers were used to spinning. By doing so, Miller believed, Whitney might be able to save the firm. While in New Haven, Miller probably also told Whitney that he and Catherine Greene would be getting married in the spring.

Certainly, Whitney must have known that the relationship between Catherine Greene and Phineas Miller was closer than that of plantation owner and manager. Miller was as free with the management of the funds of Catherine Greene's estate as he would have been if they were his own. In many senses, Greene and Miller were making official a union that already existed. Nevertheless, the news of the marriage brought home to Whitney his own lonely, debt-ridden life. He saw no immediate possibility of marriage for himself. He was not in a financial position to marry and did not feel that he could seek the company of marriageable women until he had some hope of clearing his debts and providing an income to support a family. He tried to be steadfast when his dreams of making a fortune from the cotton gin did not materialize, but the financial strain and the constant frustration were wearing him down. Throughout the next year, Whitney remained prepared to go to England. In the end, however, Miller could not find any way of raising the $1,000 needed for Whitney's voyage, and Whitney never went.

By 1796, Miller had judged the business of ginning to be a failure. He was growing desperate to settle some of Miller & Whitney's debts and to prevent a public bankruptcy. Creditors forced him to sell off some of the property from Catherine Greene's estate that he had already mortgaged. Soon after, Miller took a group of patent infringers to court, hoping to collect

Whitney's first model gin, constructed in 1793–1794 to complete his patent application, was destroyed in an 1836 fire at the federal patent office. The model gin shown here was created around 1800, and was used to defend Miller & Whitney's patent claims in court.

damages to pay off more of Miller & Whitney's debts. To Miller and Whitney's disbelief, they lost this first lawsuit in May 1797. Whitney thought the case was clear. He had taken out a patent on the cotton gin, and farmers and businessmen were reproducing and selling unlicensed copies of his patented machine. Unfortunately, it was difficult for Miller & Whitney to get a fair trial in Georgia, where so many people were profiting from the widespread use of the copied cotton

A brilliant invention does not guarantee a fortune for its inventor. A government-issued patent, or legal protection for an idea, is intended to give inventors a head start on creating a business to take advantage of their own idea. An inventor can also sell patent rights to someone else who wants to use or to sell the invention. Patents give creative people a financial incentive to invent. However, patents expire after fourteen years, because allowing an inventor to hold exclusive rights to an invention forever might hold back the development of other useful variations. An inventor who obtains a patent has the right to sue anyone who tries to copy or use the patented invention without permission during the term of the patent. The unauthorized use or production of a patented invention is known as infringement of the patent. The court will examine the inventor's claim and the infringing copy and may require the infringer to pay damages. Taking someone to court, however, can be expensive and frustrating, even if the lawsuit is eventually successful.

gins. Southern planters criticized the firm's attempts to monopolize, or take sole control of, the ginning industry, accusing Miller and Whitney of trying to cripple the South's agricultural economy to satisfy their own greed. The jury, made up of local residents, reflected this public opinion in its verdict.

In response, Phineas Miller regrouped, planned additional lawsuits, and began rethinking the Miller & Whitney business plan. Miller also had a large plantation to run, a family to care for, and several other investments and more profitable business ventures to occupy his mind. He was an established figure in Georgian society and was not without alternate means of support.

Whitney, on the other hand, was miserable. To his great embarrassment, he was indebted to creditors throughout New Haven and was worried about money all the time. He wrote to Miller to ask for money to pay and to retain the workmen hired and trained at the factory, but Miller told Whitney that he had nothing to offer but his sympathy. Unlike Miller, Whitney did not have a wife, an estate, or any other businesses or investments on which to fall back. Whitney had put all his time and energy into the cotton gin, and he felt abandoned and lost when the ginning business failed. He stopped going out in public, aware that people in town who had once remarked on his genius and his great inventiveness had begun whispering about his failure and near bankruptcy. Despite his low spirits, however, Whitney did not give up. Though he continued to fight on behalf of his patent claims in court, he came to accept that any profit from the business of cotton ginning would come too late to relieve his current financial difficulties. Whitney would see little profit from an invention that had changed North America forever.

7. Too Successful an Invention

Years after inventing the cotton gin, Eli Whitney exchanged letters with Robert Fulton, the inventor of the steamboat. As had Whitney, Fulton had watched as competing businesses copied his patented invention. Fulton had written to Whitney, asking for public support in Fulton's suit against the infringers. Reflecting on his own experiences in court, Whitney wrote, "I have always believed that I should have had no difficulty in causing my rights to be respected if [the cotton gin] had been less valuable & used only by a small portion of the community. But the use of this Machine being immensely profitable to almost every individual in the Country all were interested in trespassing. . . ." Whitney's invention was successful beyond imagining, and this would be the downfall of Miller and Whitney's business.

Whitney's patent claims were eventually upheld in court, but these victories came only after many years of litigation. In 1801, Whitney and Miller learned that South Carolina hoped to protect the state's growing cotton industry and avoid any future lawsuits by settling the matter in a single court case. Miller, acknowledging Whitney's skills as a negotiator, asked him to travel south and press their case. Unfortunately, Phineas Miller died in 1803, after a brief illness. Whitney was left to continue the fight alone. He succeeded in selling a license for the use of the cotton gin to the citizens of South Carolina for $50,000, but Whitney had to travel south several more times to press negotiations before the state actually paid the licensing fee in full in 1805.

Whitney finally had the satisfaction of seeing his right to the cotton gin upheld in Georgia, but not until December 1807, a month after the expiration of his fourteen-year patent. The case did him no good financially, but it helped to establish publicly the importance of his invention. In his decision in favor of Miller & Whitney, the judge wrote about the amazing transformation of the South during the fourteen years since Whitney's invention. The judge observed, "The whole interior of the Southern states was languishing, and its inhabitants emigrating, for want of some object . . . to employ their industry, when the invention of this machine at once . . . set the whole country in active motion." The spread of cotton agriculture in America, remarked upon by the judge and made possible by the invention of the cotton gin, transformed both the South and the North in ways that Eli Whitney could never have imagined.

Because growing cotton was profitable, the plantation system spread across Georgia and South Carolina and into new territories, including the land that makes up modern-day Alabama and Mississippi. With the spread of the plantation system and its nearly limitless demand for labor, the practice of slavery in America also spread and prospered. As the cotton industry grew, the country as a whole came to have a financial stake in the practice of slavery.

In the North, a successful textile industry grew, dependent on the inexpensive cotton that was planted, harvested, and ginned by slaves in the South. In the years after Whitney's invention, the number of textile mills in New England grew rapidly, transforming the

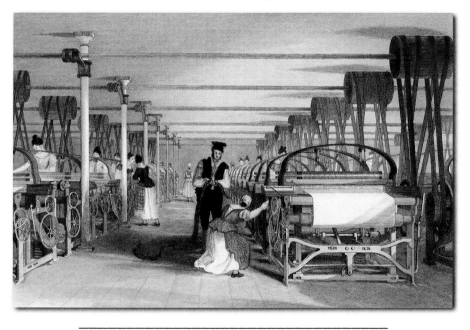

America's first mill for spinning yarn was built by English mechanic Samuel Slater in Rhode Island, in 1793. Slater employed inexpensive child labor and realized great profits. His success encouraged the founding of other mills across the northeast, creating a great demand for southern-grown cotton. This engraving by T. Allom and J. Tingle, from Slater's 1836 memoir, shows the mill's power looms at work.

economy of the region. Factories employed women and children, and provided an alternative to farming. More northern families moved from the country to the towns and cities that were built around factories. Soon the nation was roughly divided between the rural southerners who grew cotton and other crops and the city-dwelling northerners who produced textiles and other manufactured goods. These conditions helped to create the tensions between the South and the North that erupted into the Civil War in 1861.

In addition to triggering dramatic political and economic changes, the rise of the cotton industry that resulted from Whitney's invention changed what every American was wearing. Before the cotton gin launched the American production of cotton, which in turn jump-started the American textile industry, most Americans had very little clothing. The most common textile produced by Americans was made from a plant called flax, which could be broken down into a fiber and made into linen. Making flax into cloth, however, required a great deal of effort and yielded only a small amount of coarse cloth, known as homespun. Most cotton cloth, as well as finer quality wool and linen, was imported from Britain at a great expense. Consequently, only the wealthiest Americans could afford to have a lot of clothing. The rest

Previous spread: This hand-colored woodcut of slaves picking cotton was published in several periodicals during the late nineteenth century, accompanied by articles describing the lives of southern slaves.

This engraved fashion plate appeared in *Godey's Lady's Book* in 1847. With Eli Whitney's redesign of the cotton gin, the development of large-scale cotton plantations, and the growth of the textile industry, women's fashions became more elaborate, incorporating more fabric and decorative details.

of the population had only a few simple garments. After the invention of the cotton gin and the resulting rise of the American cotton industry, the price of cotton cloth fell dramatically. By 1850, most women could afford to wear dresses that used almost four times as much cloth as those that were fashionable in 1800. Clothing still was not as easy to come by as it is today, but for the first time store-bought cloth was affordable for the average American.

8. Guns and Government Contracts

Throughout the American Revolution, the patriot army's lack of muskets limited the army's efforts to build an effective fighting force. As General George Washington wrote in a letter from the battlefield, he and his troops were "in the greatest Distress here for Arms without the most distant prospect of obtaining a Supply." Washington knew that the problem was not a lack of money with which to buy guns but a lack of guns in the country, which was a more difficult problem to solve.

American gunsmiths existed, but they had small businesses, each producing less than one hundred guns per year. As the independence movement in the American colonies grew more threatening, the British government forbade British merchants to sell arms to the American colonies. Once war broke out, the powerful British navy blockaded American ports, trying to prevent shipments of European arms from getting through. France and the Netherlands provided a limited supply of guns and transported them on ships that managed to sneak past the British blockade.

A colonial gunsmith was a skilled craftsman, able to shape iron, carve wood, cast brass, and engrave metals with simple tools. A gunsmith, working with an assistant, would complete one gun in all its detail and then start another, making production slow. The machine shown here was used to polish and decorate the exterior of the gun barrel.

When the American Revolution came to an end in 1783, many Americans felt grateful to the French for the money, military expertise, and arms that France had provided during the war. The United States would probably not have gained its freedom from Great Britain without the help of France. However, the new United States needed to cultivate foreign trade with both Great Britain and France. The United States was struggling to find a balance in political relations with the two countries, who were traditionally enemies of each other. Instabilities in Europe made America's neutral position difficult to maintain. In 1789, the French Revolution began. At first many Americans were sympathetic, but as the violent Revolution continued many Americans began to question the wisdom of supporting revolutionary France. In 1793, France declared war on Britain. Britain responded with a wartime policy of seizing all ships attempting to trade with France or French colonies in the West Indies, which severely affected America and American trade. Worse, the British would sometimes take Americans from these ships and force them to serve in the British navy, a practice known as impressment.

American outrage had little effect. In truth, European diplomats were not taking America seriously. In 1794, a skilled diplomat named John Jay negotiated a treaty with Britain to help keep American trade with Britain and its colonies open. American diplomats in France were having a much more difficult time in negotiation, and Jay's Treaty, which was ratified in 1796, did not help. Relations with France worsened. Agents of the French minister of foreign affairs, known in diplomatic documents by code names X, Y, and Z, suggested to the American ambassadors that France would declare war on the United States unless the United States paid a quarter of a million dollars to the French government. Reports of this demand, known as the XYZ Affair, shocked American citizens, inspiring the slogan

to convince Wolcott to give him a government contract. He had never made a gun, but he did already have a factory of tools, and workmen whom he wished to keep employed. In his letter, he proposed to apply his proven mechanical talents to solving the government's arms shortage. He told Wolcott that he could make ten thousand muskets in the two years allowed by the contracts. No other private contractor claimed to be able to make nearly that many guns. It took twenty-six other contractors to promise the remaining thirty thousand muskets.

Whitney's first contract, for a total of ten thousand muskets, was approved with incredible speed, because war with France appeared to pose an immediate threat. By the end of May, Wolcott had written back and invited Whitney to Philadelphia, and, by June 14, Whitney had traveled there and the contract had been signed. He promised to deliver four thousand guns by September 1799, and the remaining six thousand by June 1800. The guns would be inspected by a government official at the government's expense to make sure they were well made, and any gun that did not pass inspection would not count toward the total ten thousand. Whitney would be paid a total of $134,000.

Whitney returned to New Haven with two 1763 Charleville muskets, the most common French gun used

---

Opposite: The government quickly signed Eli Whitney's contract, shown here. Only later did he confide his growing doubts to his old friend Josiah Stebbins. Whitney wrote, "I have now taken a serious task upon myself & I fear a greater one than is in the power of any man to perform in the given time—but it is too late to go back."

Articles of Agreement made on

fourteenth day of June One thousand seven
hundred and Ninety Eight.— Between Oliver
Wolcott Esquire Secretary of the Treasury, for and on
behalf of the United States of America of the
one Part, and Eli Whitney of New Haven in the
— State of Connecticut of the other Part.

1st.   The said Eli Whitney, Contracts and engages to
manufacture within the United States, and deliver
to such person or persons as shall be appointed by
the Secretary of the Treasury, or the Secretary of War,
for the time being, Ten thousand Stands of Arms,
ie Muskets with Bayonets and Ramrods complete
fit for service, Four thousand stands of which arms
shall be delivered on or before the last day of September One thousand seven hundred and Ninety
Nine, and Six thousand additional stands, on or
before the last day of September One thousand
eight hundred.

2nd.   The said Arms shall be delivered at New Haven
in the State of Connecticut. and shall be made after
the Charleville model.— The Barrels shall be proved and
the Muskets inspected, agreeable to the Rules now
practiced and required by the United States.— The
Locks shall be duly hardened.— The Ramrods and
Bayonets shall be tempered.— and the Mountings, Stocks
and every other particular shall be furnished in a
Workmanlike manner.— in all parts precisely or as
near as possible, conformably to two patterns which
have been marked and sealed by the Contracting parties
to this Instrument: two of which patterns the party of
— the second part hereby acknowledges to have received.

3rd.   The Barrels shall be proved and the Muskets in=
spected at New Haven aforesaid by a person or persons

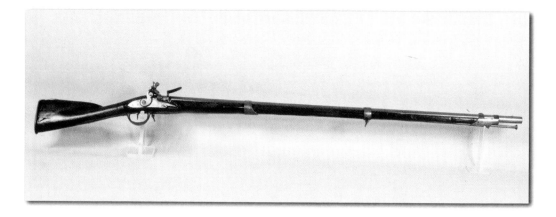

The French-made Charleville musket was the gun most commonly used by Continental troops during the American Revolution. Though it was inaccurate, slow to load, and heavy by later standards, the Charleville was a reliable and familiar weapon, and the American government felt comfortable using it as a standard. A 1795 Charleville musket is shown above.

by Americans during the Revolution and the government's model musket for contracted gunsmiths. He began studying the Charleville muskets, taking them apart and imagining how to go about making such a gun in quantity. By August, he received his first advance of $5,000, and, in November, he wrote to his friend Josiah Stebbins about the great relief he felt for the first time in years. He had had nearly $4,000 in debts with no way to repay them, and the government contract, as he wrote Stebbins, had saved him from utter ruin.

9. Making Guns Without Gunsmiths

A musket consists of three main parts: a wooden stock, or handle, that is braced against the shoulder when the musket is fired; a lock made up of interconnected metal parts, including a trigger for firing the gun and a mechanism for causing a charge of gunpowder to catch fire; and a metal barrel where the gunpowder and a lead musket ball are loaded. When the trigger is pulled, the pressure from the contained explosion of gunpowder sends the musket ball shooting out of the barrel at a target.

Finding a way to make each of these parts was not a problem in itself. One experienced gunsmith, perhaps with a few assistants, would shape the wood, form the metal barrel, work each lock part into rough shape, and then file the parts until they fit together smoothly. A gunsmith spent years learning how to do each of these different, precise operations, and very few people managed to learn all the necessary skills. However, the demand for greater gun production forced Whitney and other manufacturers to rethink this method of making guns. Skilled labor was scarce in America around 1800. Few

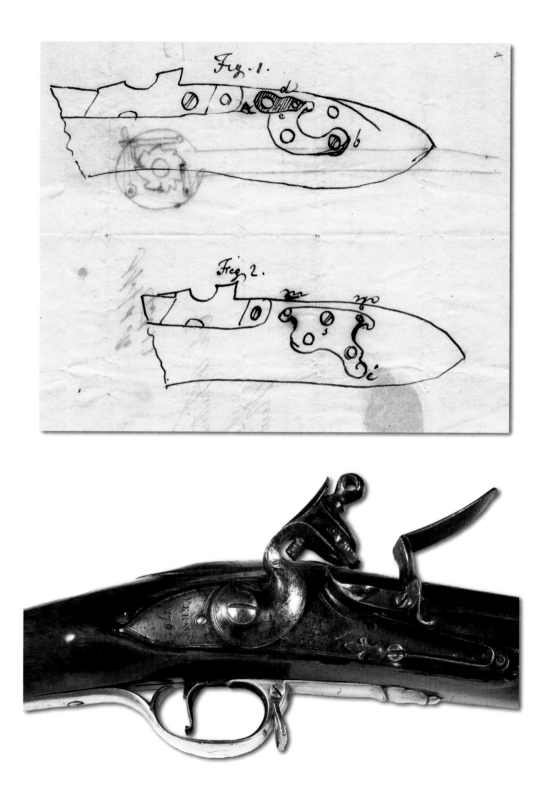

apprenticeships or other training for young craftsmen were available, and skilled workmen from other countries were not yet settling in America in large numbers.

Whitney saw the labor shortage as his primary obstacle. In a letter to Secretary Wolcott, Whitney bluntly stated that he had "not only Arms but a large proportion of the Armourers to make." He was devising a system of organizing his factory that would allow him to begin production with just a few skilled workmen and a larger group of unskilled men. Whitney realized he could quickly train the unskilled workers to perform a particular aspect of the production process, rather than investing years in the workers' development. Skilled workmen would have to be employed to shape the gun barrels and stocks, so Whitney decided to focus his ingenuity on the making of the lock, a complicated mechanism consisting of about fifty irregularly shaped parts. Whitney hoped to design machines that would allow an unskilled person to shape each different lock part perfectly. The machine and its fixtures would determine the shape of the part. The worker could learn how to use the machine much more quickly than he could learn to shape the part without the machine's assistance.

Whitney had already chosen a place to build his gun factory. A factory located by a waterfall or a rapid could

---

Opposite: Though they required the craftsmanship of skilled workers, the gun barrel and the stock were relatively simple to make, each consisting of one carefully shaped piece. The gun lock, however, was a complicated machine with many components *(bottom)*. Eli Whitney studied the parts of the gun lock and diagrammed its plates and screws *(top)*.

save labor by using the force of falling water to drive the repetitive motions of machinery. For his gun factory, Whitney found a former mill north of New Haven, a place where the Mill River ran over an outcropping of rock and made a natural waterfall. In September 1798, Whitney used his signed government contract to guarantee his purchase of the mill and the farm next door. One of the farm buildings was transformed into a boardinghouse with several bedrooms and a shared dining room, and Whitney moved in alongside his workmen. In the winter of 1799, Whitney wrote to Josiah Stebbins with excitement about the completion of his first factory building.

Whitney worked out a novel system for running an armory. In 1798, he had never made a gun. To meet the demands of his contract, he would have to learn the business and then go about reinventing it entirely. Whitney, along with other American armorers, experimented with a system of specialization that would reduce the need for skilled workers. In Britain and elsewhere, gunsmiths had shared the job of making a gun between several workers, dividing the work based on the part of the gun. For example, in a British gun shop, one man might make only triggers. Making a trigger, however, required shaping the trigger at the forge, cutting it down to rough shape, filing it to more precise shape, and

Previous spread: Eli Whitney chose to build his factory 2 miles (3.2 km) north of the center of New Haven, along what became the main turnpike to the city of Hartford. George Henry Durrie created this painting of the Connecticut countryside, with Whitney's Armory in the distance, in 1847.

Whitney's armory had a forging shop on one side of the Mill River. A waterwheel powered mechanical bellows, which blew air on forge fires to keep them hot. To forge parts for the lock, a workman would have heated an iron bar over a hot fire, then pounded it into shape on an anvil. The forged parts would be taken across the river to the machine and filing shop for precise shaping. A second waterwheel powered this shop, where Whitney eventually purchased or invented machines for cutting, drilling, and polishing the parts of the lock. The waterwheel was connected by gears to rotating metal bars that ran across the ceiling of the shop. Each machine that required power was connected to one of these rotating bars by a leather belt. The sounds of the turning waterwheel, gears, and overhead bars and the noises of metal being cut and drilled would have been loud. Even more noise came from a shop in the back, where waterpower was probably used to drive trip hammers that assisted in welding barrels together. While these early power tools did some of the work, the parts would be carefully filed before they fit together perfectly. Workmen used filing jigs to file parts down to shape. The jig determined the shape of the part, and the filer could remove excess metal until the part conformed to the shape of the jig.

polishing it to a smooth surface. The trigger maker would have to know how to do each task. Whitney and his contemporaries were working toward dividing the steps of production and assigning them to workers based on the nature of the work rather than the part of the gun being worked on. The tasks of forging, cutting, filing, and polishing the parts would each be done by a separate, highly specialized laborer.

Whitney designed machines to do the work of each of these steps, but he put even more energy into retaining his workers. He was aware of the investment that he was making in each person whom he trained. To add to

This machine, known as the Whitneyville Milling Machine, is believed to be the oldest American milling machine in existence. It was built between 1827 and 1835, modeled on an earlier design by Eli Whitney. It was in use at the armory until the 1880s, when the factory was sold and the machine was removed from the site.

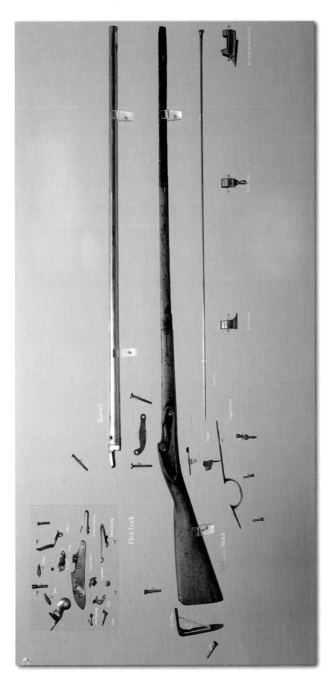

This musket, a copy of the Charleville design, was manufactured at Eli Whitney's armory in 1798. The musket has been disassembled, and its parts have been arranged in a case currently on display at the Eli Whitney Museum in New Haven, Connecticut.

Whitney's concerns as an employer, a person who did have skills generally preferred to be independent, not to work for someone else. Everyone hoped to better their situation by moving somewhere else. A talented mechanic would move from shop to shop, getting a thorough education by working in a number of different places, in hopes of one day going into business for himself. This probably benefited American manufacturing as a whole by spreading innovations from shop to shop, but it was a constant problem for Whitney and other factory owners. To keep his workers at the armory, Whitney made agreements with other armorers not to hire one another's workers, and several times he wrote letters insisting on the return of a worker who had gone off to another factory.

Whitney also tried to create a little village around the factory where workers could settle. Whitney invested his time in training apprentices, young boys whose families would sign a contract with Whitney, trading their sons' labor in return for the education that they would receive in Whitney's business. Whitney educated his own nephews as apprentices at the armory. He provided a boardinghouse for apprentices and unmarried workers, but also sought out married workers or those with family ties, which would encourage them to stay in the area. He built a row of houses across the road from the factory where workmen could live with their families. Whitneyville, as it was called, was an early predecessor of nineteenth- and twentieth-century company towns.

10. The Idea of Interchangeable Parts

By the terms of his agreement with the government, Whitney should have delivered his first four thousand muskets by the fall of 1799. He was nowhere close to meeting the deadline. Overoptimism on the government's part and perhaps desperation on Whitney's part contributed to these unreasonable expectations. In 1798, the government wanted to believe that it could solve its musket shortage quickly. War with France seemed possible at any moment. Whitney told the government what it wanted to hear in order to get the contract that he so badly needed to make a new start. Both parties entered into a contract that they should have known was impossible to complete in the given time frame. Even the federal armory at Springfield, Massachusetts, had taken about five years to get its tools, machinery, and workmen in order and to reach full production levels. Whitney took ten years to finish what he had said he would do in two. The last of the muskets owed under his 1798 contract would not be delivered until 1808.

Beginning in 1799, Whitney sent letters to Secretary Wolcott, trying to justify the delay in the delivery of the muskets he had promised. He made some commonplace excuses about unforeseeable difficulties with the weather, but he also started promoting an idea that captured the imagination of several government officials and helped to secure the extraordinarily long extension of Whitney's contract. Whitney claimed that he needed additional time because he was attempting to make uniform parts that could be interchanged between one musket and another.

Today, if a person buys a car and a part of the engine ceases to function, that person can order a replacement from the company who made the car. A mechanic can remove the part that is broken and install the new part in its place without modifying the part or the engine. The car will function with the new part. This repair is possible because all the cars of that model and year have parts that are uniform. Every cylinder, valve, and piston in the engine is exactly the same as the cylinders, valves, and pistons made for the other cars. A car engine is a complicated machine, but because car engines are made of interchangeable parts they can be produced and repaired very efficiently. Teams of workers and machines make just one kind of part and can do it quickly. A final team can put together all the parts into a working engine, and it does not matter which parts end up in

In summer 1798, yellow fever gripped the nation's capital, Philadelphia, closing federal offices and interrupting trade. The next winter, snow-storms halted production and trade across the northeast. Eli Whitney needed iron, steel, and gunstocks. Above all he needed time and money. He wrote to Oliver Wolcott and asked for an extension. A page from one of Whitney's letters to Wolcott appears above.

which engine because all of the parts of a certain kind are the same.

In Whitney's day, complicated machines were not made this way, but he could imagine a day when they would be, and he helped to convince the U.S. government of the benefits of this process. In December 1800, nine months before he finally delivered the first five hundred muskets owed on his contract, Whitney traveled to the nation's new capital, Washington, D.C., to demonstrate the idea of interchangeable parts to a group of War Department and other important government officials, including the outgoing president, John

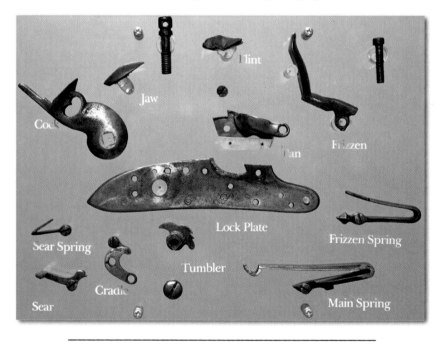

Eli Whitney's old friend and tutor, Congressman Elizur Goodrich, described the response to Whitney's demonstration in Washington: "All Judges & Inspectors unite in a declaration that [Whitney's muskets] are superior to any which the artists of this Country, or importation have brought into the Arsenals of the United States." The interchangeable parts of a Whitneyville-made lock are shown here.

Adams, and the president-elect, Thomas Jefferson. Whitney brought with him the unassembled parts for ten muskets. He placed them in a pile on the table and then assembled ten muskets from randomly selected parts, suggesting that the musket parts being made at the Whitney Armory were so similar that it did not matter which parts went together in which gun.

Some people did not see the value of the idea of interchangeable parts. A French arms maker had developed guns with uniform parts in the 1780s. It appeared to have taken him so much time and effort that skeptics thought the pursuit of uniform parts in gunmaking was financially impractical, even though it might offer interesting benefits yet to be realized. Some people, however, were captivated by the idea. Eventually, the U.S. government became convinced that striving for uniformity in parts would improve the American production of guns. By measuring the precise size and shape of each part before assembling the whole musket, assembly could be made more efficient and the number of arms that failed inspection could be reduced. Many years after Whitney's demonstration in Washington, making arms with interchangeable parts became a priority at the Springfield Armory.

Modern studies of Whitney's guns have revealed a surprising truth, however. When the locks of muskets made at the Whitney Armory are taken apart, it becomes clear that the parts are not entirely uniform.

Making uniform parts requires the ability to measure the dimensions of each part with precision. In Whitney's day, the difference in size between two parts considered uniform was generally no more than $\frac{1}{32}$ inch (0.8 mm). Special brass tools for measuring small differences existed in Whitney's time, but they were expensive and would not have been found in most industrial workshops. Instead, Whitney's workmen compared their muskets with the parts of the 1763 Charleville muskets that they had been given as models. Unfortunately, after being held up for comparison next to the parts of a few thousand muskets, the parts of the model musket would show wear, getting smaller and changing shape. The new parts being made would reflect these undesirable changes. Government inspectors had a different method for examining the finished guns. They carried sets of gauges, which had spaces that matched the dimensions of a model musket. These gauges were used to judge the shape and size of each gun part. By 1819, these gauges were being used in the workshop of the Federal Armory at Springfield. Workers tested the parts with the gauges as they worked on them, not just during inspection. These were important steps toward achieving part uniformity and interchangeability.

For 174 years, the federal armory at Springfield, Massachusetts, was the center of American small arms manufacturing. The armory stopped production in 1968. Today the main arsenal building, shown above, houses a weapons museum.

They cannot be put in piles and assembled into locks at random, as Whitney did in his presentation in 1801. In fact, each part had tiny letters stamped on it to help the gunmaker remember which parts went together in which lock. Whitney must have specially prepared the parts he used for his demonstration. The parts made at his factory were not, in general, interchangeable.

Achieving the goal of interchangeable parts would require advances in every area of shop practice. Methods of cutting and shaping parts had to be made easier to control. Tools for measuring the size and shape of things had to be improved and made available to workers. Changes had to be made in the way that workers were trained and the way in which their work was organized. Neither Whitney nor any other individual can be said to have invented or single-handedly achieved interchangeable parts. However, Whitney believed it was a possibility, and he worked toward this goal. Both arms makers and War Department officials understood the need to cooperate, and, in 1815, Whitney hosted a meeting with a number of government officials and superintendents from different armories for the purpose of discussing methods for making gun parts uniform. Achieving uniformity, as the skeptics had predicted, cost a great deal and took decades. In the end, the federal armory at Springfield was the institution best able to invest the years needed to make the innovations in machine tools and shop practice necessary to achieve uniformity, which it accomplished in 1849.

Whitney worked toward the achievement of interchangeable parts in several ways. He planted the seed that would help to shape the government's political commitment to interchangeable parts, and his promotion of the idea helped to make the challenge of uniformity a priority goal at the federal armory at Springfield. Whitney, who had worked to systematize the way his workmen made cotton gins, also strove for systematization in his gun factory, and he spread his ideas through the apprentices and superintendents who worked with him and then moved on to other factories. In particular, Whitney shared ideas with Roswell Lee, a mechanic and gifted administrator who lived in New Haven and worked with Whitney before becoming superintendent of Springfield Armory in 1815. It was under Lee that Springfield Armory began working seriously toward the goal of uniformity.

11. Whitney's Legacy

In 1797, Whitney had been lonely and deeply in debt, writing with anguish about his limited prospects for marrying and his failed business. By 1810, he and his workmen were making two thousand guns per year, more than two hundred times the output of early American gunsmithing businesses. In 1812, when war broke out between Great Britain and the United States and the government made a new round of contracts with Whitney and other arms makers, he had a fairly secure business as a gunmaker. Whitney was beginning to acquire a respectable amount of wealth, primarily by investing his modest profits from the armory and the cotton gin patent licenses in real estate and other ventures. He had an enduring reputation as an inventive genius. He had met on more than one occasion with U.S. presidents. Yet he was living with his workmen in a boardinghouse at his factory, and, although he participated in the upbringing of his nephews and other young apprentices, he had no family of his own beyond the family of employees and ever-changing housekeepers who cooked his meals.

He remained close to Catherine Greene even after Phineas Miller's death. She wrote him frequently, urging

President James Madison signed a declaration of war against Great Britain in June 1812, beginning the War of 1812. Americans resented Britain's oppressive maritime presence and Britain's involvement in the U.S.-Indian conflict. Native Americans had resisted the spread of white settlement, and Britain had provided military support to the Indians. This engraving by Alonzo Chappel shows British soldiers in battle.

him to visit her in Georgia and commenting on his health like a concerned mother. Whitney even considered proposing marriage to one of her daughters, but such a union never came about. In 1814, he learned that Catherine had died after a brief fever. He mourned for an extended period of time. In 1817, Whitney married Henrietta Edwards, who came from a well-respected New England family. Her father was a longtime business associate of Whitney's who had helped to guarantee the purchase of the gun factory site. Fifty-one-year-old

Whitney moved out of the boardinghouse and into a rented house in town with Henrietta. Over the next few years, the couple welcomed two daughters and a son into their family. Whitney purchased some land and made plans to build his family a grand house, but illness and physical weakness, the effects of years of hard work and stress, began to overtake him.

Whitney left instructions in his will for the house to be built for his widow, and, in 1825, Whitney died. His nephews, whom he had trained as apprentices, ran the armory with success until Whitney's son, Eli, came of age and took over the business in the 1840s. Young Eli

Before his death, Eli Whitney studied his declining physical condition, reading medical journals and textbooks. He even invented and built instruments to treat his illness, but the exact details of these tools were never recorded. His condition was incurable. This headstone marks Whitney's grave in Grove Street Cemetery, New Haven, Connecticut.

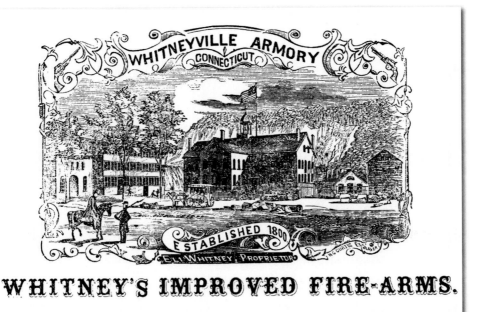

WHITNEYVILLE ARMORY
CONNECTICUT

ESTABLISHED 1800
ELI WHITNEY, PROPRIETOR

WHITNEY'S IMPROVED FIRE-ARMS.

By the late nineteenth century, Eli Whitney's armory had grown significantly. It employed more laborers and produced several different kinds of guns. The armory completed its last government contract just after the end of the Civil War and went on to develop pistols and rifles for the commercial market, making advertisements, including the one shown here, a necessity. M. C. Curtis engraved this image of the armory.

ran the armory until 1888, taking the business through the Civil War and a number of significant changes in gun technology. The armory at Whitneyville thrived, and factories throughout the North adopted the elder Whitney's methods of production.

Eli Whitney Jr. was a solid citizen and a successful businessman in his own right. In fact, it was during the younger Eli's lifetime that the elder Whitney's vision of systematized, uniform industry was finally realized.

Yet Eli Jr.'s accomplishments were largely overshadowed by those of his famous father.

•   •   •   •   •

It is Eli Whitney's curious legacy to have been an important figure in both the rise of cotton production in the South and the development of an industrialized economy in the North. As such, he was at the center of the tensions that fostered the outbreak of the American Civil War. Yet Eli Whitney's impact on American life extended beyond the war, particularly

Eli Whitney Jr. tore down many of the armory's original buildings to expand his business and to make room for a new, larger dam. The dam was built for the New Haven Water Company, which was owned in part by Eli Jr. Later industries used the armory site to make stoves, wires, and industrial ceramics. Today the site, shown above, is a museum.

in the North, where the first great modern cities grew up around the early factory towns.

Eli Whitney is best remembered for the flash of genius that brought the world the modern cotton gin, but for most of his life he worked on developing the structure of American industry. The ideas developed by Eli Whitney and his contemporaries about how to organize a factory and make the parts of a machine uniform were eventually applied to and improved in other industries that required precisely shaped parts, such as the manufacture of sewing machines, bicycles, and typewriters. In 1851, a fair was held in London to showcase the products of many different countries. The American exhibit created a stir. American products such as a revolver made by Samuel Colt and farm machinery made by Cyrus McCormick were judged to be better and more efficiently made than products from anywhere else in the world. The United States had proved itself to be a leader in world manufacturing.

Timeline

1765	On December 8, Eli Whitney is born in Westborough, Massachusetts.
1775	Unrest in the colonies erupts into the American Revolution.
1777	On August 8, Eli Whitney's mother, ill since the birth of her fourth child seven years earlier, dies when Eli is eleven years old.
1779	On June 12, Eli Whitney's father marries widow Judith Hazeldon, who has two daughters of her own.
1781	The British surrender at Yorktown leads to the end of the land war of the American Revolution.
1785	Eli Whitney announces his intention to attend college and takes a winter job teaching school in Grafton, Massachusetts.
1786	Eli Whitney, age twenty, begins study at Leicester Academy during the spring and summer to prepare for college.
1786–1789	Whitney continues to work as a schoolmaster in the winter and to study at Leicester during the summer while trying to convince his family to pay for his college education.
1789	On April 30, Whitney interviews with Yale's president, Ezra Stiles, in New Haven, Connecticut, and successfully earns admission to Yale College. On July 14, the French Revolution begins with the storming of the Bastille in Paris.
1792	Eli Whitney graduates from Yale College.

| | During October and November, Eli Whitney travels to New York and then to Savannah, Georgia, with the intention of taking a position as a tutor at a southern plantation. Instead, during a stay at the plantation of his traveling companions, he invents the cotton gin. |

1793 In June, Whitney begins applying for a patent on the cotton gin. He completes the application the following March, but the patent is backdated to November 6, 1793.

1794 During May and June, Whitney returns to Georgia with cotton gins he has built in New Haven. Phineas Miller and Eli Whitney sign partnership papers, officially establishing the cotton ginning business of Miller & Whitney.

1795 In March, fire destroys the main building of Whitney's cotton gin factory in New Haven.

1796 In May, Phineas Miller and Catherine Greene are married in Philadelphia. Later that year, Miller sues competitors and patent infringers who are making and selling gins.

In November, the American treaty with Britain negotiated by John Jay is ratified, which enrages France. Three American diplomats are sent to France to attempt to negotiate.

1797 In May, Miller and Whitney are defeated in their first patent lawsuit.

1798 In April, the release in America of the reports of the American negotiators in France spurs American outrage against France. Congress arranges private contracts for the manufacture of muskets.

On June 14, Eli Whitney contracts with the U.S. government to build ten thousand muskets in two years.

1801 In September, Whitney learns that the state of South Carolina may be willing to purchase patent rights for the cotton gin. He travels south to represent Miller & Whitney in the decision, a trip he repeats several times during other patent right negotiations over the next five years.

1803   On December 7, Phineas Miller dies at the age of 39. Whitney travels to Georgia to visit his widow, Catherine Greene Miller.

1805   In July, the firm of Miller & Whitney receives complete payment for the sale of the right to use the patent gin to the citizens of South Carolina. The patent on the cotton gin, which had a term of 14 years, expires in November of 1807.

1808   Whitney completes his 1798 contract for ten thousand muskets.

1812–1815   The United States declares war on Britain. The War of 1812 stimulates demand for arms and spurs reorganization of the war department and the way it handles arms contracts.

1812   Whitney receives a second government contract, this time for fifteen thousand muskets.

1814   Catherine Greene Miller dies at age 61.

1815   Superintendents from various armories, including the Federal Armory at Springfield, meet at the Whitney Armory with government officials to discuss methods for making gun parts uniform.

1817   Eli Whitney marries Henrietta Edwards. In the coming years, Henrietta and Eli would have two daughters and a son.

1825   Eli Whitney dies at the age of 59.

Glossary

apprenticeships (uh-PREN-tis-ships) Periods in which young people work with experienced people to learn a skill or a trade.

bankruptcy (BANK-rup-see) Official declaration by a person or business of an inability to pay money that is owed, resulting in legal proceedings and loss of property.

blockade (blah-KAYD) Ships that block passage to ports by ships of another country.

capacity (kuh-PA-sih-tee) The total amount that someone or something can make or hold.

cash crop (KASH KROP) An agricultural product grown primarily for market.

creditors (KREH-dih-turz) People to whom money or goods are owed.

cylinder (SIH-len-der) A tube-like object.

damages (DA-mij-ez) In a lawsuit, money awarded by a judge to a plaintiff, or person with a complaint, to be paid by a defendant.

entrepreneurs (on-truh-pruh-NURZ) Businesspeople who start their own businesses.

firm (FERM) A company or a business.

forge (FORJ) A workshop for heating and shaping metal.

guineas (GIH-neez) Units of British money that were used between 1663 and 1813.

homespun (HOHM-spun) A loosely woven fabric.

inoculation (ih-nah-kyoo-LAY-shun) The injection of infected cells into the body of a healthy person with the hope of causing a mild case of the disease and future immunity.

mentor (MEN-tor) A trusted guide or teacher.

micrometer (my-KRAH-meh-ter) An instrument for measuring very small units of length.

mortgage (MOR-gihj) An agreement to use a piece of property as security for a loan; if the loan is not paid back, the lender gets to keep the property.

muskets (MUS-kits) Long-barreled firearms used by soldiers before the invention of the rifle.

negotiator (nih-GOH-shee-ayt-er) Someone who tries to reach an agreement between different people.

packet ship (PA-kit SHIP) A sailing ship specially designed to carry passengers and small amounts of cargo.

patent (PA-tint) An official document that gives an inventor the right to sue people who steal the patented invention.

plantation (plan-TAY-shun) A very large farm. During the 1700s and the 1800s, many plantation owners used slaves to work on these farms.

revolver (rih-VOL-ver) A handgun.

specialization (speh-shuh-lih-ZAY-shun) Adaptations for a particular kind of work.

stagecoach (STAYJ-kohch) A horse-drawn vehicle.

superintendents (soo-puh-rin-TEN-dents) People who oversee others' work.

textile (TEK-styl) Woven fabric or cloth.

tribute (TRIH-byoot) Money paid by one country to another in surrender or for protection.

tuition (tuh-WIH-shen) The price of instruction at an academic institution.

tutors (TOO-terz) People who teach one student or a small group of students.

Additional Resources

To learn more about Eli Whitney and the history of American manufacturing, check out these books and Web sites:

Books

Hakim, Joy. *The New Nation 1789-1850: A History of US, Book 4*. New York: Oxford University Press, 1993.

Macaulay, David. *Mill*. Boston: Houghton Mifflin, 1983.

Shuter, Jane, ed. *Charles Ball and American Slavery*. Austin, TX: Raintree Steck-Vaughn Co. Publishers, 1995.

Web Sites

Due to the changing nature of Internet links, PowerPlus Books has developed an online list of Web sites related to the subject of this book. This site is updated regularly. Please use this link to access the list:
www.powerkidslinks.com/lalt/ewhitney/

Bibliography

Deyrup, Felicia Johnson. "Arms Makers of the Connecticut Valley: A Regional Study of the Economic Development of the Small Arms Industry, 1798–1870." *Smith College Studies in History*, vol. XXXIII. Smith College: Northampton, MA, 1948.

Federico, P. J. "Records of Eli Whitney's Cotton Gin Patent." *Technology and Culture* 1(2), Spring 1960.

Hall, Karyl Lee Kibler and Carolyn Cooper. *Windows on the Works: Industry on the Eli Whitney Site 1798–1979.* Hamden, CT: Eli Whitney Museum, 1984.

Hilliard, Sam B. "Plantations and the Molding of the Southern Landscape," in Michael P. Conzen, ed., *The Making of the American Landscape.* New York: Routledge, 1994.

Kaestle, Carl F. *Pillars of the Republic: Common Schools and American Society, 1780–1860.* New York: Hill & Wang, 1983.

Mirsky, Jeannette and Allan Nevins. *The World of Eli Whitney.* New York: Macmillan, 1952.

Raber, Michael S. "Conservative Innovators, Military Small Arms and Industrial History at Springfield Armory, 1794–1918." *Industrial Archaeology* 14 (1988).

Smith, Merritt Roe. "Eli Whitney and the American System of Manufacturing." in Carroll W. Pursell Jr., ed., *Technology in America: A History of Individuals and Ideas.* Cambridge: MIT Press.

Vaughan, Harold Cecil. *The XYZ Affair, 1797–98: The Diplomacy of the Adams Administration and an Undeclared War with France.* New York: Franklin Watts, Inc, 1972.

Woodbury, Robert S. "The Legend of Eli Whitney and Interchangeable Parts." *Technology and Culture* 1 no. 3, (1960).

Index

About the Author

Regan Huff is an educator and a writer who spent time working, teaching, and doing archaeological research at the museum that is now on the site of Eli Whitney's gun factory in Connecticut. She enjoyed getting to know Eli Whitney, his son, and the workers at their factory through the letters that they wrote, the account books that they kept, and the guns and other artifacts that they left behind.

Primary Sources

Cover, p. 4. *Eli Whitney*, oil on canvas, circa 1822, Samuel Finley Breese Morse, New Haven Colony Historical Society. **Page 10**. Map of colonial America, labeled "To the Hone. Jno. Hancock, Esqre. president of ye Continental congress, this map of the seat of civil war in America, is respectfully inscribed by his most obedient humble servant, B. Romans," created in 1775, Bernard Romans, from the Geography and Map Division of the Library of Congress. **Page 14**. The Lyons Farm Schoolhouse, which was built in 1784, stands at the intersection of Chancellor and Elizabeth Avenues in Newark, Essex County, New Jersey. **Page 15**. Whitney's writing sample, entitled "To the Selectmen of Westbrorough," pen and watercolor on paper, 1786, part of the Eli Whitney Papers, held by the Manuscripts and Archives, Yale University Library. **Page 17**. Leicester Academy, engraving, held by the Paul E. Swan Library, Becker College. **Page 20**. *Reverend Ezra Stiles*, oil on canvas, 1794, Reuben Moulthrop, Redwood Library Painting Collection. **Page 21**. *A view of the Buildings of Yale College at New Haven*, etching, circa 1910, based on an engraving by A. P. Doolittle, © Corbis. **Page 23**. Microscope, 1734, manufactured by Mathew Loft, held by the Historical Scientific Instruments Collection at the Yale Peabody Museum. **Page 24**. Yale University's Connecticut Hall, completed circa 1757, photograph held by the Prints and Photographs Division of the Library of Congress. **Page 27**. Signature of Phineas Miller from a letter he wrote to Eli Whitney on September 20, 1792, held by the Eli Whitney Papers, Manuscripts and Archives, Yale University Library. **Page 28**. Map of the United States, engraving, 1785, by William Faden, Library of Congress Geography and Map Division. **Page 30**. *A View of Broad Street, Wall Street, and the City Hall*, watercolor, 1797, John Joseph Holland, held by the Phelps Stokes Collection, Miriam and Ira D. Wallach Division of Art, Prints, and Photographs, at the New York Public Library, Astor, Lenox, and Tilden Foundations. **Page 31**. *Catherine Littlefield Greene*, oil on canvas, James Frothingham, Telfair Museum of Art. **Page 34**. Rice cultivation, mid-nineteenth century, artist unknown. **Page 37**. Woman beating cassava, watercolor and gray ink, created between 1808 and 1816, William Berryman, Library of Congress Prints and Photographs Division. **Page 39**. This cotton gin belongs to the National Museum of American History, Smithsonian Institution. **Page 42**. Eli Whitney's sketch of the cotton gin for his patent application, graphite, ink, and watercolor on paper, dated March 14, 1794, held by the

National Archives and Records Administration. **Page 45**. Partnership agreement between Eli Whitney and Phineas Miller, part of the Eli Whitney Papers, Manuscripts and Archives, Yale University Library. **Page 48**. Phineas Miller's advertisment in the *Gazette of the State of Georgia*, dated March 1, 1794, part of the Eli Whitney Papers, Manuscripts and Archives, Yale University Library. **Page 49**. A letter written by Thomas Jefferson to Eli Whitney, dated November 16, 1793, part of the Eli Whitney Papers, Manuscripts, Yale University Library. **Page 55**. Demonstration model of Whitney's cotton gin, held by the Division of Social History, Textiles, National Museum of American History, Smithsonian Institution. **Page 61**. A power loom at work, hand-colored engraving, drawn by T. Allom and engraved by J. Tingle, printed in *Memoir of Samuel Slater, the Father of American Manufactures*, written by George Savage White and published in 1836, held by Rosen Publishing. **Page 62–63**. Slaves picking cotton, hand-colored woodcut, published in 1880, North Wind Picture Archives. **Page 65**. "Godey's Paris Fashions Americanised," published in *Godey's Lady's Book*, Culver Pictures. **Page 68**. A machine for grinding, polishing, and decorating the exterior of gun barrels, engraving, mid-eighteenth century, published in Diderot's *Pictorial Encyclopedia*, Dover Pictorial Archive Series. **Page 73**. Eli Whitney's first government contract to manufacture guns, dated June 14, 1798, part of the Eli Whitney Papers, Manuscripts and Archives, Yale University Library. **Page 76 (top)**. "...Explanation of an improvement made in the Musket Lock by E. Whitney, 1816," ink and graphite on paper, held by the Eli Whitney Papers, Manuscripts and Archives, Yale University Library. **Page 76 (bottom)**. Detail of a Brown Bess flintlock musket, late eighteenth century, part of the George C. Neumann Collection, Valley Forge National Historical Park. **Page 78-79**. *Ithiel Town's Truss Bridge*, oil on canvas, 1847, George Henry Durrie, New Haven Colony Historical Society. **Page 82**. Eli Whitney's milling machine, known as the "Whitneyville Milling Machine," created circa 1827–1835, held by the New Haven Colony Historical Society. **Page 83**. Exploded musket on display at the Eli Whitney Museum, New Haven, Connecticut. **Page 87**. A letter from Eli Whitney to Secretary of Treasury Oliver Wolcott, part of the Eli Whitney papers, Manuscripts and Archives, Yale University Library. **Page 91**. The Federal Armory at Springfield, Massachusetts. **Page 95**. *Death of General Ross*, engraving, mid-nineteenth century, Alonzo Chappel. Chappel's engraving shows British soldiers but, because Chappel did not have British firearms to refer to, the muskets the soldiers carry are in the style of American-made muskets of the period. **Page 96**. Eli Whitney's gravestone, Grove Street Cemtery, New Haven, Connecticut. **Page 97**. Advertisement for Whitney firearms, circa 1862, Library of Congress, Prints and Photograph Division.

Credits

Photo Credits

Cover (portrait), pp. 4, 78–79, 82 New Haven Colony Historical Society; cover (background image), p. 42 National Archives and Records Administration; p. 9 Colonial Williamsburg Foundation; pp. 10, 28 Library of Congress Geography and Map Division Washington; pp. 14, 24, 37, 97 Library of Congress Prints and Photographs Division; pp. 15, 27, 45, 48, 49, 73, 76 (top), 87 Eli Whitney Papers, Manuscripts and Archives, Yale University Library; p. 17 Courtesy Becker College; p. 20 Redwood Library Painting Collection; p. 21 © CORBIS; p. 23 © Yale Peabody Museum; p. 30 the Phelps Stokes Collection, Miriam and Ira D. Wallach Division of Art, Prints, and Photographs, the New York Public Library, Astor, Lenox, and Tilden Foundations; p. 31 Telfair Museum of Art; pp. 34, 65 Culver Pictures; pp. 39, 55 Division of Social History, Textiles, National Museum of American History, Smithsonian Institution; pp. 62–63 North Wind Pictures; p. 68 Dover Picture Archives; p. 74 Guilford Courthouse National Military Park; p. 76 (bottom) The George C. Neumann Collection, Valley Forge National Historical Park, photo by Cindy Reiman; pp. 83, 88, 98 The Eli Whitney Museum; p. 91 by David Stansbury; p. 95 Anne S. K. Brown Military Collection, Brown University; p. 96 © David Reiman.

Project Editor
Gillian Houghton

Series Design
Laura Murawski

Layout Design
Corinne L. Jacob

Photo Researcher
Jeffrey Wendt

BPMS MEDIA CENTER